Hiding under the Blanket

By

Dorothy A. James

Dedication

To all my children

Anthony, Lashaunda,

Tammy, Ivan,

and Stephanie

Acknowledgment

I would like to give special thanks to:

My Lord and Savior, Jesus Christ, who has taught me the importance of forgiveness (Matthew 6:14-15).

Truly if it had not been for the Lord on my side I would have lost heart (Psalm 27:13).

My Lord and Savior, has provided a place in His word for me to be cultivated and to answer to the call that He has mandated upon my life, and to help other women to be set free and delivered. I encourage you to continue in prayer, and to trust God. Because He

says in His Word, He will "never leave you nor forsake you".
(Hebrews 13:5).

I will always have a love for who He is to me, not for just what he can do for me. My service to Him is not an option. It's just my reasonable service. My personal experience with God in prayer, faith, and trusting Him has increased and changed my life forever. It will change yours too, if you make Him your choice and do things His way.

Contents

Introduction

In today's society, there are many attacks on the Body of Christ. We often read and hear scandalous rumors of pastors engaging in infidelity and money mismanagement, but seldom do you hear of pastors who abuse their wives. Sadly, what we call "the church," a place that should be for healing and restoration, has become a place with hidden secrets of sinful behaviors that are too horrible to mention.

This book has been written to share a portion of my life testimony on how God delivered me from the hand of my abuser and to encourage those who suffer or may know someone who is suffering the same or maybe worse situation. I pray that these words help those victims to stop *hiding under the blanket* of physical, verbal, sexual, and emotional abuse and live to behold the beauties of our Lord and Savior, Jesus Christ.

Women, I am still here because of Christ. I suffered physical, verbal and emotional abuse from my ex-husband who is a pastor. Many times, I came close to death's door at the hand of my abuser. He drew a gun on me several times, choked me until I passed out, stomped me and he even dragged me like a rag doll. He knocked me down as though I was some type of boxer in a ring. Yet, I was the one being defeated. I can recall nearly being drowned and having many other horrendous things done to me.

I am so glad that one day I chose to wake up and get out before it was too late for me and I became a statistic at the morgue. God did not make me to be a doormat or carpet to be walked or trampled upon. He made me as His precious jewel to be loved and cherished.

God sees you and me as the apple of His eye **(Psalm 17:8)**. In other words, we are greatly valued and dear to Him. He sees you and me as this phenomenal woman that He created us to be.

For I know the plans I have for you," declares the Lord, "Plans to prosper you and not to harm you, plans to give you hope and a future." **(Jeremiah 29:11).**

I want you to know that I made an intelligent decision to stop taking punches and blows from my abuser that said he loved me, that kind of love I never want again from any man. Now, come journey with me into a portion of my life story.

Chapter One
A Portion of My Life's Story

My name is Dorothy and I am a woman that God created. I do not present myself as one who was the perfect wife, who never offended my ex-husband, nor was I submissive to his authority in every area. Although, I made every effort to love, cherish and respect him as being the head in our home, as in many homes, this was not the case. What is most important is that I loved him for over 31 years in the truest sense of fidelity. I was never separated from my husband, always being faithful to him with my mind, body and heart – even though I was accused of unfaithfulness repeatedly. I had to realize that nothing that I did or did not do deserved to be treated in this manner by a man that said he was called to preach by God. I had been *hiding under the blanket* by living secretly with physical, verbal, and emotional abuse for 31 years.

Although my abuse took place during the time I was a married woman, this message applies to the married and the unmarried alike. As you read through my horrifying story, I pray that the Lord will help you to see a total life transformation from fear and dread to peace and joy. Also, I pray that you will experience the same conversion and be strengthened to help another woman to stop hiding under the blanket.

Psalms 27:13 (NKJ)
[13] *I would have lost heart,* unless I had
believed
that I would see the goodness of
the LORD
In the land of the living.

Chapter Two
My Disobedience to God

I found myself being disobedient
to God when He had allowed me to get
away from my abuser, but I continued
to return time and time again. Then I
begin to question God as to why He was
allowing this to happen to me, but I had
to face the truth. It wasn't God doing it.
It was my own disobedience because
God's Word said to me in *(Proverbs
21:2), "Every way of a man is right in his
own eyes, But the LORD weighs the
hearts"*.

Even though I found myself at a place of disobedience God still had compassion on me and delivered me. I want you to know that He will deliver you as well. However, you must trust Him for who He is and for what His promised Word says.

When the devil tried to beat me over my head with pain, shame and disappointment I could tell him that I am an overcomer because of Christ, and I said to him, "Get thee hence behind me Satan, I no longer live by your threats, but by every word that proceeds out of the mouth of God according to *(Matthew 4:4)* *He answered and said, "It is written, man shall not live by bread alone, but by every word that proceeds from the mouth of God."*

I give all the honor and glory to God for what He has done in my life. He has kept me for such a time as this to share with you His love and His mercy. Inside of you is the ministry of reconciliation just as He has given me. I continue to pray for my abuser because of the God that is in me. I have a destiny to come to for God's purpose in accordance with

(Philippians 1:6) Being confident of this very thing, that He who has begun a good work in you will complete it until the day of Jesus Christ".

Even as Christ brought Joseph to the very purpose he was born for, Joseph did not allow unforgiveness to set in his heart against his brothers for abusing him. He showed the love of Christ for them and helped them, he was in compliance with *(Philippians 2:4) "Let each of you look out not only for his own interests, but also for the interests of others". (i.e. the offender or abuser).*

I had to come to the understanding that my past fears would hinder me from moving forward so, I decided I could not allow this to happen.

I had to talk to myself and meditate on what God's Word says about me and not listen to the lies of the devil. God has spared my life and kept me for such a time as this to encourage women all over the world with this learning experience, because "never been there can't tell the story".

All of this has worked for my good because God has made me a living testimony for his glory. According to *(Romans 8:28) which says,* *"And we know that all things work together for good to those who love God, to those who are the called according to His purpose".* God removed the low self-esteem that I once had about myself. Because of how He sees me and his thoughts toward me, I am God's phenomenal woman and so are you. *(Jeremiah 29:11) "For I know the thoughts that I think toward you", says the*

LORD, *"thoughts of peace, and not of evil, to give you an expected end"*.

God sees me as the apple of his eye. I am remarkable, extraordinary, impressive, outstanding, astonishing, unbelievable, incredible, astounding, exceptional, unique, unusual, rare, and extra special, not just ordinary.

In addition, I am fantastic, marvelous, wonderful, amazing, brilliant and great. These are his distinguishing qualities that He has placed inside of me and he would not have me any other way. It is all for his good pleasure. This is what my God has done for a woman like me both inside and out. I am encouraged and I want to encourage you to know that God "will never leave you nor for forsake you". *(Hebrews 13:5).* This is his promised Word to me and to you.

Chapter Three
Forgiveness is God's Method

First and foremost, I give honor to my Lord and Savior Jesus Christ who spared my life and brought me out. I want to share the forgiveness that God placed in my heart for my abuser. As you read this book, I pray that you sense the heartbeat of my intentions, that I am about to convey to you. As those different events that took place in my life, I did not have the mind at first to forgive my abuser.

However, God brought me to the understanding that I had to forgive if I wanted His forgiveness. I knew that I wanted God's mercy and His forgiveness to be applied towards me so I had to do the same towards my abuser. I had to continue to pray and ask God to change my mindset and think the way He wanted me to think. Because unforgiveness would have hindered me from going forth and being all that I could be for God, I made an intelligent decision to humble myself and allow God to do the exalting. He spoke His Word to me to put on His mind. According to *(Philippians 2:5),"* *Let this mind be in you which was also in Christ Jesus, and (James 4:10)," Humble yourselves in the presence of the Lord, and He will exalt you"*.

God's method to forgive said to me in *(Matthew 6:14-15)*

14 " For if you forgive others for their transgressions, your heavenly Father will also forgive you".

15 "But if you do not forgive others, then your Father will not forgive your transgressions".

Therefore, forgiveness is essential. These verses are a must regardless of your feelings. I had to believe in my heart that God is faithful to bring total healing and restoration in my life, which he did. I am a living testimony of this statement. I had to be willing to have a compassionate heart toward the abuser, even though I fell into his repentance trap and reconciled six times with him. However, I now understand that God wants to reconcile the abuser back to Himself. Only if he (the abuser) would humble himself, repent, and cry out for His help.

Chapter Four
Real Love Never Changes

One beautiful night, I met the man
with whom I thought I would spend the
rest of my life. We spent time together,
shared delicious meals and took walks
in the park getting to know each other.
We had wonderful conversations and
were able to embrace each other. We
wanted to spend more time together,
realizing that we loved each other's
company so much that we did not want
to spend another day apart. Finally, our
long desire was culminated when he

asked me to marry him. I said, "Yes," of course, as if I could ever refuse him. Feeling ecstatic and anxious to be with my love, it only took me one week to make plans for our big day. Our big day took place on December 9, 1978.

During my childbearing years, my husband was very happy to witness his sons and daughters come into the world. However, when I was pregnant with our first daughter, we got into an altercation, and he pushed me down in the closet and stomped me. We got into altercations on a regular basis. Mostly, because he accused me of infidelity for which there was no truth. As our children were born, he would follow the nurse down the hallway into the nursery, keeping a close watch on them. He would come back to me in my room and say, "They are not going to get my baby mixed up with no other baby!" Oh, the proud and happy look on his face could not be taken away from him at that hour and moment as if he was the perfect father.

As the children began to grow up, their dad loved all of them, and he protected them from any harm within his power. He was an excellent provider. He made sure they had a roof over their heads, clothes on their backs and food on the table.

For the most part, the beginning of our marriage and parenthood seemed spectacularly impressive. We experienced love on many levels. We never wanted to leave each other's side – even to go to work. He told me that he would love and take care of me for the rest of my life. I believed him. Who wouldn't? Every woman dreams of their knight in shining armor coming to rescue them from dangers seen and unseen.

During this joyful time, he showered me with many beautiful and expensive gifts of purses, clothing and jewelry. One of my most memorable gifts was a 5.2 carat, princess-cut, diamond ring. I felt so loved and cherished, as if I was a princess discovering the extent of my prince's kingdom.

My husband was also very talented and skillful in various areas.

He built us an eleven-bedroom, five-bath home that sat on a hill of splendor for all to see. We traveled around the world, flying here and there to places I would never have gone without him. I did not know that I had to pay a price for this grand life!

Soon our marriage, the sparkling glass of my glittering life, shattered. My knight in shining armor, whom I fell in love with, began to control my every move. It started with the verbal abuse, which quickly escalated to emotional and physical abuse.

The root of this abuse stemmed from a very insecure man who believed that I'd had an affair with another man. Yet, there wasn't any truth to the accusations.

I can remember back to the beginning of our marriage. I had just started working outside the home. One day, I came home after a hard day and went into the bathroom. He burst into the bathroom, snatched me off the toilet and tore off my underwear checking to see if I had been with another man. This happened on many occasions.

It was the beginning of over 30 years of fear, pain, humiliation and hurt that eventually would numb me. My self-esteem had gone out of the window. I just accepted all the abuse. Many times, I would cry out to God and ask Him why He was allowing this to happen to me when He knew I was innocent. How could I tell or let anyone know what was happening? All I could do was start hiding under the blanket, covering up what was there – pain, disappointment and shame.

Chapter Five
Love Never Acts Erratically

I didn't understand what was happening in my life. I grew up in a loving home, understanding how a man was to take care of his wife and children. My parents taught us the value and morals of life. My father and mother painted a picture that husbands and wives were to stick together and take care of the family the right way.

Yet, here I was living the exact opposite. *I Corinthians 13:5b (Amplified Version) states that it (love) is not rude, unmannerly and does not act unbecomingly"*.

I knew that this "love" was not proper because I was no longer allowed to do the norms that we practice in our society. For example, being a mother to my children in every sense of the word.

This meant so much to me because my mother taught me as a young lady how to do many things. One very important thing was her teaching me how to be business savvy. I had to learn how to pay the bills. Sometimes she would give me the correct change and sometimes she would not. She would ask questions afterwards such as, "How much money should you have gotten back?" and "What is this?" and "How much money did I give you?" Questions such as these provoked me to want to learn more and make her proud. The precious moments that I spent with my mother in the kitchen were later a part of my inspiration in writing a cookbook. She was an excellent mother. I also wanted to be an excellent mother, but my ex-husband's control and dominant behavior, hindered me from spending as much time with my children and protecting them as I desired.

There were times when their father chastised them in an abusive manner, and I hated it. Many times, he and I would bump heads on how he would discipline them. He would call them out of their names. I would say to him, "You are wrong." He needed much training in this area because he provoked our children to anger many times. The Word of God says in Ephesians 6:4, *"Fathers, provoke not your children to anger"*.

The Word of God in (Proverbs 3:5-6) teaches us to acknowledge God in all our ways and He would direct our paths. If only he had asked God to teach him how to discipline our children to not abuse them, then our children could have reflected back on lessons where discipline was essential. We could have sat down as a family and had conversations about some of our childhood experiences, lessons we both have learned from, but his controlling behavior and escalating abuse just led us down the road of brokenness. His position of pastor and preacher was more important than parenting. Although I asked him to seek counseling, he felt that no one else could tell him anything and I better not dare talk to anyone about what goes on in our home or there would be consequences. His refusal to work on changing through counseling caused me to not get a chance to build a relationship with my children while they were growing up. I did not have the opportunity to sit down and have mother-to-daughter conversations nor did he try to have father-to-son conversations because he kept me under him like I was some type of body glue made just for him.

He insisted on things been done "his way" most of the times. This type of attitude further let me know that this "love" was not of God. I Corinthians 13:5 continues to state that "Love does not insist on its own rights or its own way". This controlling behavior prevented me from connecting with my siblings and other family members that I grew up with. He tried to stop me from visiting my parents when I wanted to, but I rebelled against this type of behavior because no man was going to stop me from seeing my parents. Often, we would get into arguments about this. I refused to let a man take me away from my father and mother. Even though I struggled to stay connected with my siblings and cousins, I was no longer allowed to go to their homes. I was slowly slipping into to his paralyzing control. I did not know how to bring back the man that I loved. I did not realize that these were some of the signs of an abuser – isolation from family.

It did not just stop there. Sometimes I was not able to go to the grocery store by myself, nor was I allowed to visit other people that I knew or visit Christian sisters nor I wasn't even permitted to attend Christian retreats. I simply was not allowed to have fellowship with anyone outside of his realm of control.

Chapter Six
Distinguishing God's Love From Man's Love

Although the Scripture tells us that God's love never fails, this "love," (man's love that I had been experiencing was a lie, and it had failed. Over the next twenty plus years, I suffered abuse so horrid, that I contemplated taking my own life. As I share with you my experiences from those twenty plus years, I implore you to take a look further into what I went through and choose life.

Psalms 121:1

[1] I will lift up my eyes to the hills —
    from whence comes my help?

There was an incident where we had an altercation before Sunday service when I refused to go to church in the state of mind I was in. This was because we had gotten into it the night before, but I was still forced to go. He took out the gun and made me put on my clothes. When we got to the church, one of his members got up and stood between us and had me sit with her. He had the gun under his coat, but nothing took place at church. We did not have service. He apologized to the members, because they had come out for service, only to be told that there would not be any service on that day. The abuse continued for the rest of the day. I wasn't allowed to go downstairs to see my children or to feed them. They had to fend for themselves, and there was nothing I could do about it. I felt less than a mother and hopeless.

Then one night he made me leave our home, which was across the street from the church and our daycare business. He made me get on my knees with the gun pointing towards my head. He kept telling me to open my mouth so he could put the gun barrel in it. He demanded that I tell the truth about a man who had never been in my life. I was crying out for my life, and he made me be quiet. He then slapped me in my face and then hit me on the side of my head with his hands and fist. I kept telling God that I did not deserve to be treated this way. I was so afraid to leave my husband from the beginning of my marriage until my late forties. I endured the harsh abuse and control, carrying the pain and hurt for much too long.

There was another incident that occurred when I was knocked to the floor and stomped like a dog. Even now my little finger on my left hand doesn't stretch out like the rest of my fingers –

something that I will live with for the rest of my life.

I can recall the time when he would make me sit upstairs like I was his child and study the Bible. If I did not read it to him as he instructed me, he would jump on me shouting, that I would not disrespect his God, asking, "Do you hear me?"

Sometimes, my children would not see me when they came home from school because he made me stay upstairs. Other times, he told me that I was not eating dinner or that I was going on a fast. He would often call me fat and out of shape.

I remember one day how he jumped on me, choked me, and left marks around my neck. He jabbed the gun into my jaw so hard until the partial wire in my mouth got embedded into the side of my jaw. I could not open my mouth for three or four days to eat, brush my teeth or talk. The children were not allowed upstairs at all during those times. If they needed something, they would crack the stairway sliding door open to yell for whatever it was that they wanted.

One morning about 2 a.m., he made me get out of bed. He said that we needed to talk away from our two youngest children who still lived at home with us because he felt that I had been lying to him, and he couldn't rest around me until this matter was cleared up. I told him there was nothing to clear up because I hadn't done anything. He told me that I was lying, and I better not tell him that again or he would bust me in my face! I told him that I did not want to go anywhere because the kids were asleep and we could talk right there in the room.   He told me to get up, started pushing me down the stairs and out of the front door and said, "Let's go. Get in the Expedition."

He then drove down to the big lake in the community where we lived in Atlanta, Ga.   There he began to question me about a man from Fort Myers. He wanted to know what was going on with that picture, which was about 18 years prior. I told him nothing was going on.   He asked me why I stopped to talk with him while I was trailing behind him. I told him that was my cousin, and he said I was lying. Then he rushed from behind the wheel of the Expedition, snatched open my side of the door, and dragged me out of the vehicle and pushed and held me down under the water. I could hardly breathe and was gasping for air.

Whenever he would let me up out of the water, I would be pleading with him not to take my life. He said to me that he was going to send me to hell that night because I had played with his life and took him for granted. He continued to dunk my head in and out of the water and held me down. I was too afraid to scream for help because I would have been dead by the time any neighbors got to the lake. I was shaking like a leaf on a tree and my teeth were chattering. He pulled me out of the water and told me I better tell him' "the truth about this nigger".

At that time, I made up a lie so that my life would be spared. Even though, I did not know whether it would be spared or not, I was taking a big chance. I told him that the guy wasn't my cousin after all, and the reason why he stopped me on that day was to tell me that if he didn't treat me right to let him know about it because he heard that he went for bad. I said, "Okay, Cuz." Knowing that this person really is my relative, I lied because he preferred to accept the lie rather than the truth.

Most of the abuse took place in our hometown of Fort Myers, Florida. Later, he said that the Lord told him that we were to move away. On September

23, 2003, we moved to Atlanta, Georgia, where I was still being accused of seeing other men even in a new state. One day, I was knocked to the floor, slapped in the face, hit upside the head, and had a gun drawn on me.

Another time, I was forced into the Expedition and taken into the woods where he drew a gun on me and told me to tell the truth about men that were never a part of my life or I knew nothing about.

My life was a living nightmare being married to this monster of a man let alone a man of God. Had I chosen to give up on God and return to my old self, I knew he would have been dead a long time ago, and my children would have grown up without their mother to raise them.   I would have probably been in prison for murdering their dad.

My oldest daughter, who is now in her thirties, asked me, "Mama, why did you stay in that marriage and take all of that abuse?" I told her, "I stayed in it in my earlier years because I didn't want you all to grow up without your dad in the home. I also stayed in it because the church members did not need this type of scandal in the church or their lives and I covered your dad for the Gospel's sake". My daughter then told me, "Mama, you should have left because God would have taken care of us somehow." Then I replied to my daughter, "Now as I look back, I wish I had gotten out of the situation a long time ago."

There was another incident that took place in Atlanta. He abused me one night and then the next day he came into the bedroom, woke me up and told me to get into the Bible with him. I said to him, "I'm not getting into the Bible with you. You just abused me last night." I told him that I did not respect him. Then he dared me to tell him that again, and told me not to leave the room. So, I got on the floor and sat against the wall because he had got into the bed, and I did not want to be anywhere near him. When he fell asleep, I slipped out of the room as if I was going to the bathroom and threw my son a note letting him know that if I was not out of the room by 6 p.m., he and his sister were to quietly leave the house and call the police and tell them what was going on.

They did leave the house. When he discovered the children were gone, he came raging at me asking me where they were. I told him I did not know, since he told me not to leave the room. He took me with him to find the children. We went to one neighbor's house and they weren't there. We went to another neighbor's house and they were there, but they wouldn't come out. He told the mother of the house that he was going to call the police on her for having his children in her house without permission.

Before we could get back into the Expedition, two police cars came up and blocked us in. One of the officers called my name and asked me to come to him. My ex-husband started walking with me, and the officer told him to back up. My husband did not like that because he did not know what I was telling the officer. Then the officer asked me what was going on, and I told him and I said I wanted to get my children and leave.

He took the children and me to the house to get some of our belongings and made their dad stay outside while he escorted us inside. He took us to a hotel to stay until the next day. Then I went down to the courts to take out a Temporary Protection Order (TPO) until the court date. The judge granted the TPO.

After going through the process of leaving him, the children and I stayed at a hotel for three weeks. Then, we relocated back to Florida. After being gone from him for about a month, he realized that we were back in Florida. I gave in and gave him my phone number, and we started talking again. He was pleading and crying for me to give our marriage another chance. I gave in again, but our children did not return home with us right away because the State had intervened. Because when I got back to Florida, I contacted them about the situation in Atlanta. Although I never followed through, the State of Florida still intervened and we had to fly back and forth to court in order for me to get my two youngest children back.

I was more fearful of him than I was of God at one point in my life. He brought two church members to our home to tell them about me as though they were my judge and jury. They have always supported him whether he was wrong or right – even to this present day. These members are five women who still support him with their tithes and offerings while he preaches to them over the phone.

It's a wonder that our children still have anything to do with their dad after what he has done to them. For the most part, our children knew when their dad attacked me because they would hear us upstairs when we were living in Florida. They were in their rooms, afraid to come out. He had that kind of fear and control over the entire household. Some days my children came home from school and didn't see me until the next day because he had attacked me. Then, he did not want them to see me with the swelling and scratches in my chest and neck area.

One time my oldest daughter ran out of the house to a neighbor to call the police on their dad because he had attacked me. When the officer arrived, I protected my ex-husband by saying, "Everything is okay. We just had a few heated words. This made my oldest daughter feel bad when she was only looking out and trying to protect me.

While we were living in Atlanta, my ex-husband made me wake up our two youngest children near midnight –

knowing our children had to go to school the next day – just to tell them a lie on me. Both children were sitting on the floor, up against the wall, nodding to sleep. They were to stay awake while hearing their dad say to them, "I know you all look at me like I'm the bad person in this house, but the reason why your mom and I are always into it is because your mom has messed up in this marriage." My children did not believe him because they knew how he kept me stuck under him and controlled me. They already knew if their dad had caught me with another man, he would have killed both of us. They knew what type of person their dad was.

Our children did not get back to bed until 2 a.m. and had to get up for school at 6:30 a.m. I had to sit and not open my mouth while he was talking to our children. What a terrible life for children to endure this type of abuse and have these types of memories to stay with them for life.

During another incident while living in Atlanta, our youngest son had moved to California because he and his dad had an altercation. Then, our youngest daughter and I left their dad when he started threatening me again all because I wanted to let our daughter go to a prom. He rejected her going to the prom. When she and I moved out he did not know where to find us. He made up a lie and contacted an elderly lady that we knew back in Fort Myers. He told her that I had left him for another man. Later, she told me that he was lying because she knew what type of woman I was. "Rev.", she said, "You did not allow your wife to go anywhere,

69

even when she and I went to the store. Before we were in the store for thirty minutes, there you were calling and asking her how long before she'd be coming back home". Then, she told him not to call her again with that foolishness.

Later, he called our oldest daughter and told her that he saw me and our youngest daughter leaving out of a hotel with a man. She told her dad "You are lying because we know what kind of man you are, if you would have seen our mom and another man coming out of a hotel you would have killed them both".

He told her he had the tape to prove it, since he had videotaped us. She said, "Send the tape to me." But he never produced a tape because he was lying once again. I was too afraid to try and get help for us to come from under this type situation because he told me more than once, "Before I let you leave me, I will kill you!"

When youngest daughter went to Florida to spend Christmas with her siblings, I joined an exercise class. One day when I returned home, I went into the bathroom to take a shower. My ex-husband came into the bathroom questioning me about a phone call that came to our home supposedly from a man. When he said, "Hello," the man hung up. I didn't believe that because those phone calls always happened when I was sleeping or at the gym. He kept asking me who were all these niggers that kept calling the house phone and his cell phone? I would then say to him that I didn't know anything about a man calling. When I asked him who are these men asking for when they called, not one time did he tell me that a man called and asked for me by my name. He just accused me of being involved with them no matter what I said.

He would tell me to come clean or he would kill me and send me to hell. I kept telling him I had nothing to do with any of those phone calls, and then he snatched open the shower door and pulled me out. I fell, and when I got up, he slapped me and said, "Nigger, you are lying to me!" He then flung me around on the wet floor hitting me repeatedly. I fell on a big glass jar of decorative marbles and my head hit the jar, breaking it.

I was bleeding badly and my head began to hurt. There was so much blood in the bathroom that I knew I needed to get to the hospital and get stitches. But my ex-husband would not take me, nor would he allow me to take myself or to call for an ambulance. He pushed me back into the shower and turned the water all the way to cold. However, I could not stay under the cold water. I soaked up big bath towels of blood from my head. Then when I started cleaning up the blood I kept wondering where it was still coming from. I looked down at my right hand, just above my thumb and saw that my flesh was open, it was bleeding badly, and hurting.

I could see the pink in my hand, and I was afraid to close my eyes that night because I didn't know if I would die in my sleep because of the blood loss. It took me a while to bring the bleeding under control. This scar on my hand and head will be there for the rest of my life. My hand bothers me from time to time, making it hard for me to use it because of the pain.

During that time, whenever I would go to the bathroom and look into the mirror, I would cry or feel hatred inside of me toward this man because of what he did to me. Finally, I built up the enough courage to leave him after we had another big blow-up. I took my youngest child and left him. I called the police to help us get out. The next business day, I went to the courts to take out a TPO against him and the judge granted it. I moved in with a neighbor for a short period of time. I started looking for a job so that my daughter and I could find us a place to live. I found a job and an apartment within two weeks.

Then, we were scheduled to go to court to establish visitation for my ex-husband, and it was granted. I had to take my daughter to the police station for him to get her for weekends or for a day. He would send messages through our daughter, and I gave in and allowed him to have my phone number. He began calling me every night. I told him that I did not want to talk to him that often. Yet, I allowed him to talk me back into coming back to him after two months.

Once again, I fell for his repentance trap. Also, I fell back into a controlled situation again after hoping that things would be better after two months had passed. At that time, I had been married for 28 years and still was going through the drama and foolishness in my life. I still was on a rollercoaster ride that looked like it would never end. This was a very insecure man, and I became his target and his punching bag of choice.

All hell broke loose again with my husband claiming that a man called his cell phone and hung up. Of course, he was saying the man was trying to reach me. Again, there was no truth in this.

Again, he threatened me by saying that he was going to kill me. This made me afraid for my life. I had to plan to get away somehow to a neighbor's house to call the police. My youngest daughter and I left and stayed at a hotel for a while, and then we moved into a shelter.

After a period of time, I went back to him, hoping that things would change. In 2007, he had to take me to the hospital, and I was hospitalized overnight for chest pains. I think it was from all the stress in my life - going back and forth through this repeated cycle of abuse.

Then, we relocated from Atlanta to Meridian, Mississippi. Once again, he said the Lord told us to move there.

But the real truth was he was running from the shame of facing the neighbors in the community because I had called the police out to our home several times. I asked him to go with me to a pastor for counseling. He did not think one was good enough to minister to him. This has always been a problem for him.

After relocating to Mississippi, we got settled in, and sometimes men would call the landline phone and some of them would say they have the wrong number and sometimes the caller would just hang up. It didn't matter. I was told by my husband that the men were calling for me, which was never true.

I have been choked, hit repeatedly, knocked around like a rag doll, not able to use the phone and not able to go anywhere. Whenever our children called to talk to me, I was forced to put the phone on speaker so he could hear our conversation. He carried his cell phone and mine in his pocket whenever we went off together. He gave it to me to call our children only in his presence. I was treated like a young teenager, not as an adult. I was living in toleration, which was a nightmare for me.

On December 23, 2007, our youngest son came home from California to visit us for the Christmas holidays. I was trying to act as if everything was okay and not alert him of anything because I did not want his holiday to be ruined. I was still hiding under the blanket, covering his dad's wrong deeds.

After our son left on January 5th, 2008, going back to California, the control started up again. It began with my husband telling me to call my job and tell them I would not be coming back on the day I was scheduled to work. I had to obey his command without any say in the matter at all. I was being controlled by a man who has lost all self control and sense of order and reality. I still did not know how to get out, how to become free because I was so depressed and oppressed that I essentially gave up my will to fight. I was tired. I had no support, and I needed the help of the Lord.

While in of Mississippi, my husband choked me. I did not report this to the authorities because he would not let me go out the door or use the phone. He kept me in his presence at all times. When he left the house, he made me go with him. Again, it was regarding a man supposedly calling me and phone calls coming in which I had nothing to do with or knew nothing about.

Another problem we had while living in Atlanta and Mississippi occurred when I was made to get up at

2:00, 3:00, 4:00 and 5:00 – all in the wee hours of the morning – to study and help edit programs for my ex-husband's internet ministry. Of course, I had an attitude about being awakened at that time of morning, who wouldn't?

June 12, 2009, three of our grandchildren came up to visit for the summer, but their stay was cut very short. We took them back to Florida after two and a half weeks. My ex-husband and I had a big argument about me spending $350 at the grocery store, which included groceries for the daycare and for the family. He was raging mad about that and I told him that he never said anything before, why now? However, he had other things on his mind such as going over previous years of credit card statements to see if anything was linked to me and a man at a hotel. The fire was really being fueled for more of his abusive behavior and control.

I was in the living room, and he was in the bedroom, when he called for me to come to him. He had me to call our daughter so she could get the children from around this foolishness. I went to my side of the bed to get my purse to take my phonebook out to call her and he demanded that I stay in the bedroom to make the call. When I started dialing, he slapped the phone and the phone book out of my hand. Then he started up again asking me, who was these niggers I have had in our marriage, and began calling me a whore that was running around from hotel to hotel in Atlanta. I said to him that I had not been running around with men, nor had I ever been outside of our marriage.

Then he said to me that I had taken his and his children's inheritance from them by whoring around. I said to him that I have not been whoring around. He told me to shut up and to stop my lying and sit down.

At this point, he had provoked me to anger. Then he told me to lower my voice in his house. When he asked me if I heard him, I said, "Um-hum," and he said, "Answer me!" Then he hit me in the face, and saddled across me as if I were a horse.

Around 2:30 a.m., he choked me until I passed out. At first, when I came to, I didn't know what had happened to me, since he wasn't in the room. He returned and told me to stand up, and he asked me again why was I lying to him, and I told him I was not lying to him. He then told me not to tell him that again, and he slapped me in the face and knocked me on the floor and choked me again until I passed out for the second time. When I came to that time, I could not move my body. It was as if something happened to my body functions. I was like a person who had a stroke and wasn't able to do anything for myself for about three hours. It was like my body was lifeless, yet he was demanding for me to get off the floor.

He went out of the bedroom for a while, and when he returned he told me to get up off the floor in a demanding way. I slowly with a slurred speech told him I couldn't move. Then he said to me, "I don't feel sorry for you." I remained slumped over on one side against the wall. He walked out of the room again and came back and saw me still in the same position. I guess he started feeling remorseful or afraid that I was going to die because he picked me up off the floor and put me in the bed. But I couldn't move myself over in the bed. He had to push me over, and I could not lift my head off of the bed to straighten up the pillow behind my neck. He had to lift my head up to make me comfortable. I was afraid. Tears were rolling down my face, and I could not lift my hands to wipe the tears out of my face, nor could I pull the cover over my body. He had to do that.

Just at the break of dawn, my body began to start back functioning properly. What a horrifying situation to be in. Yet, God was still with me just as He was with Joseph. He did not permit me to die at the hands of my ex-husband.

When we returned back from Florida, we went out to the pasture to take care of our horses. We had a bitter conversation on the way there. He said to me again, that my children and I don't have an inheritance because of my whoring. I said to him, "I have not been whoring with anyone." He replied, "Tell me that again. Do you hear me talking to you?" I just said, "Um-hum." He did not like my reply and he told me I'd better open my mouth and answer him right. He told me at the farm that he would slap the hell out of me. Then someone that we knew came up to the fence and started talking with him briefly.

He got out of the Expedition and went to the gate to open it so that he could feed the horses. He decided to ride one of them, so I stayed in the vehicle. He told me to get out while he saddled up the horse and continued to argue. He then told me to get in the truck and ride alongside him as he rode the horse, and I did. I had every opportunity to leave him at the farm, but I waited. When we left the farm, I drove back to town and stopped at Wal-Mart to return a movie to the Red Box. When he got out and went into the building, that was my time to get away from him. I drove right to the police department and took out a warrant for his arrest for threatening me. I knew once he got me back home into the building no one would be able to hear me when he started fighting me, and if I screamed, I would not be heard either, so I did not want to take that chance. I had taken enough chances with my life being married to this insecure man. Then, I moved into a women's shelter until our court date. Once the court date was set, I went to court, the judge ordered my ex-husband to stay away from me for twelve months.

I began preparing to relocate back to Florida where my family were living.

I really had to pray and believe that God would take care of me in my transition from Mississippi to Florida. God knew what my life had been like being married to this man of God who called himself a pastor. God spoke to me that He would be my shelter in the time of a storm because He is my refuge according to Psalms 71:7.

I moved back to Fort Myers only to have him continue to beg, cry and plead for me to come back to him. Then, I fell into his repentance trap again. My husband kept trying to contact me through our daughter, asking me to please call him. Finally, I did. He told me he did not know why I had left him. He continued to beg and plead for me to come back to him. I told him, "Right now I need to seek God."

He continued to hound, plead, and beg for me to come back to him. Then he flew down to Florida. I was praying to the Lord and asking what He wanted me to do. The third day the Lord spoke to me and said, "Wait patiently on me," Psalms 27:14. Yet, I moved ahead of God and went back into the same situation. I regretted it afterwards as I found myself moving back again.

I encourage you to heed the voice of God and to not be pressured by man. After I fell into his repentance trap, I moved back to Mississippi again. Little by little, along the way, the control started again in my life.

I was still being dictated to, controlled and dominated like a puppet on a string by this man who calls himself a preacher. This was the same man that I'd been married to for 31 long years of my life.

December 9, 2009, was our 31st wedding anniversary. He did not remember it. I did not tell him because it meant nothing to me anymore. There was nothing for me to celebrate. It was only when our grand-daughter called to wish us a happy anniversary, that he remembered and thanked her.

I came home from work at the daycare and got settled in, he asked why I didn't say anything today about our anniversary. I told him that I should not have to remind him of our anniversary. We both knew what date it was. After all, it wasn't a big deal with me. When he asked me to go to dinner after 9:00 at night, I told him no. He had an attitude, but I did not care. He did not understand that I had stopped loving him long time a ago.

On Monday, December 21st, 2009, I was running the daycare business and he started dictating me again. I told him I was sick and tired of him and this foolishness in my life. I was going to give the parents two weeks' notice that I was closing the center down permanently. He told me, "No, you're going to let them know today!" So, I replied, "Okay. I will get the letters ready and call them on their jobs." I hated doing these parents and children like this, but I wasn't given much of a choice.

My ex-husband told me not to threaten him with closing the daycare business, and I told him, "It's not a threat. I closed it down once, and I will do it again." He said to me, "If you do, let's take it all the way." I asked him,

"What do you mean?" And he said, "Let's go to my attorney and wrap up this divorce." And I replied, "Let's do it."

I finally woke up and came to my senses. I came from hiding under the blanket meaning I would no longer stay hidden under the blanket while he is abused and controlled me as he stood before God's people preaching to them. It was past the time for exposure and for the cover to come off him. On Tuesday, December 22, 2009, I proudly went in and signed the divorce papers without hesitation. I did not fight for the material stuff we had accumulated over the years. I just wanted out and to have peace in my life and to feel that I have a life. God gave me the right to can make decisions, my own decisions. It was never his will for man to take what He died for. He didn't give me life to allow it to be taken by man. On Wednesday, December 23, 2009, I relocated back to Fort Myers where my family members were living once and for all, I was not going to fooled by his repentance trap any more.

As I was driving the thirteen hours back to Fort Myers, crossing over the Mississippi – Alabama Stateline, my middle daughter called to check on me. I told her that I was fine. Before we hung up with each other, I told her, "I will be exiting the bridge on my next exit to fill up the truck." After we ended our conversation, the Spirit of the Lord spoke to me and told me, "Get off at the upcoming exit." It's never wrong to heed the voice of God because it's for your own good according to Romans 8:28.

I was driving a 14ft U-Haul truck with an attached auto transport carrying the car on top. When I exited off the expressway and came to a gas station, I made a startling discovery – the whole tire was missing off the auto transport that was carrying the car. Out of my mouth came praise to God for protecting me from danger. Not one time did I murmur or complain. I cried because he had spared my life and took care of me. The Word of God says in *I Thessalonians 5:18 to give thanks in all things* (and that's what I did). *God's assigned angels protected me – Psalms 34:7.*

I am happier now than I've ever been in 31 years of my life has been a living hell from the age of 18 to 50. I am no longer bound, no more chains holding me. Thank God, I'm free at last, free at last, thank God Almighty I'm free at last, thank God!

I truly thank God for taking care of me through it was all because He told me in His Word that He would never leave me nor forsake me. I have made the right choice even though it was 31 years later. This is why I wanted to share my story in hopes that other pastors' wives, married women and unmarried women who can relate to my story would come from hiding from under the blanket and let these men be exposed. I personally presently know a few pastors' wives, married and unmarried women who are living in this kind of situation. This is not the will of God for your life! Women, do not continue to live like this. Don't be deceived by their repentance trap like I was. Don't allow precious years of your life to go by without doing something about it! Women, get up come out and trust God to take care of you because you are that "phenomenal woman".

After leaving my ex-husband once and for all, God's Word spoke to me and according to Psalms 118:17, "I shall not die, but live and declare God's work."

Women, I want you to know God has allowed me to live to tell the story so that your broken hearts can be healed. Also, you can proclaim liberty once again. You are no longer held captive at the hand of your abuser. He has caused your prison doors to open and you are no longer bound, no more chains of abuse in any form will be holding you down. Know that God will cause you to bounce back and you will spring forth again. Praise God! Praise God!

In my closing of this book, now that God has healed and set me free, I am an extremely happy and vibrant woman again. My hope in God has caused me to be able to love again even after 31 years of a bad marriage, because

God has given me that hope. If you saw me then and you see me now I don't look like what I been through only because of Christ and he saw fit that I shall not die, but live, and declare his works (Psalm 118:17).

To all those that may or may not be in an abusive relationship. Whether it's emotional, physical, verbal, or psychological. I would like to encourage you to contact the abuse hotline:

1-800-334-2836 or 1-800-96-Abuse

This book gives vivid details of my journey as a pastor's wife when I was hiding under the blanket of shame, fear, depression and pain for 31 years and how my loving Savior, Jesus Christ, rescued me and made me a phenomenal woman! I want you to know out of all my pain that I went through, I found my purpose which was to bring this message to you.

Now it is your turn women to come out of the grip of abuse, and let the healing begin.

''I believe this book will be a life changing book for all women that will dare to trust God.''

Dorothy A. James

God's Process to forgive never fails **(Ephesians 4:32).** Do not allow your past hurts to hinder your future.

The Father has called for His children to get acquainted with Him through seeking His face which is His Word and prayer.
In His Word is where deliverance and restoration starts.

Made in the USA
Columbia, SC
25 February 2025

54417661R00063